The Attic

Finding the Treasure in Your Tragedy

Renita Johnson

Copyright © 2015 Renita Johnson
All rights reserved. This book or any portion thereof may not be reproduced or used in any manner whatsoever without the express written permission of the publisher except for the use of brief quotations in a book review.

Renita Johnson
renita@ladyjhelps.com
www.ladyjhelps.com

Limits of Liability and Disclaimer of Warranty

Although the author and publisher have made every effort to ensure that the information in this book was correct at press time, the author and publisher do not assume and hereby disclaim any liability to any party for any loss, damage, or disruption caused by errors or omissions, whether such errors or omissions result from negligence, accident, or any other cause. Views expressed in this publication do not necessarily reflect the views of the publisher.

I have tried to recreate events, locales and conversations from my memories of them. Some names and identifying details have been changed to protect the privacy of individuals.

Printed in the United States of America

ISBN 978-1-941749-21-0

4-P Publishing

Chattanooga, TN 37411

Cover Illustration Copyright © 2015 by Melony Collins
Cover design by Melony Collins
Editing by Keen Vision Editing, LLC
Author photograph by Melony Collins
Poetry of Renita Johnson

Printed in the United States of America

4-P Publishing

Chattanooga, TN 37411

Acknowledgements/Dedication

God blessed me with so many people who walked along side me on my journey to healing. Some were there for a season and some were there my entire life. To each of you, I am indebted. Thank you for your time, patience, love, and endurance.
 A Special Thanks to:
My Parents, Doris and the late Nathaniel Carter
My Step Mom, whom I truly adored the late Dallas Carter
My Sister, who I love, respect and admire Robbie Carter
My Brother, who taught me how to fight and take a few punches, the late Nathaniel Carter Jr
My Sister, Deborah who would give you the shirt from her own back
My Sister, Phyllis thank you a million times over for introducing me to my soul mate, Lemont Johnson.
My Baby Sister, Michelle thank you for continuing to pray and believe that I would make a comeback! I admire the humble and quiet spirit you possess.
My entire set of nieces, nephews, cousins, step siblings and in-laws. I have much love and appreciation for you.
My Dear Aunt, the late Lavern Harden, you are missed greatly.
My wonderful Taccoa, GA family, thanks for all the great summertime memories and family reunions. I will never forget the great love you all showed me.
Nicole, Tiffany, Nikki and Denita, you all are my jewels.
My name sake, Vernita, no worries we will make it.
My loving Step Parents, Janice and Tommie Pruitt you both stepped to the plate and helped me through one of the hardest times of my life. Thank you Jan, you are still coming through for

me. I just love you guys!

My prayer warrior, the late Evangelist Betty Ryan Ringer, she had a great love for my family.

Dr. Belva, Fai Smith, Pastor Walter Cross, Pastor Holloway, along with your lovely wife. You all were used in a mighty way during the early process of my healing. Thank you, I am forever grateful!

To Darwin Randolph, thank you for your prayers. You always said I could do this. Pastor Sheryl, I admire your ability to keep pushing, Thanks for seeing potential in me. I appreciate your encouragement, thanks for all the positive things you have spoken into my life. I love me some you!

My friend and sister, Gwen Davis from Sunday school, to the hospital days, and the beauty shop, whew! Thanks for teaching me how to have grace and show grace to others. You had a lot of grace when it came to loving me. Thanks big sis.

Special thanks to Pastor Kevin and Lady Cynthia Adams for their love towards Kesha during her transition. Pastor Kevin, thank you so much for your encouraging words, "just simply start, put the pen to paper and you will accomplish your book!"

If I call you friend, you had to do the "go through" with me.

Special, Roll Call: Diane and Sharon, you both made the cut. I value our long friendship and school days.

Veronica Beasley and Sandra Parker, the challenges of the hospital days. I know you all love me. I was truly in the raw. Thank you for all your patience.

Angie and Yvonne, prayer time was essential. I am thankful for every Saturday morning we spent! What a commitment we had to God and each other! Thanks for the love.

Terry Ramsey, I can hear your soft voice saying "Renita, don't let nobody pull your string." Well, I finally got it. It would not have been possible without you walking with me and encouraging me to be loving and kind towards Kesha during the time when she worked my last nerve. I love you for your tender ways. Thank you. Love to all the beauty shop gang: Wilma, Cheryl, Willene, Gayle, Nan, Janelle, Nikki, Carmen, Nieka, Toya, Ronda, Natalie, Gwen, Marsha, Fai, and Juanita just to name a few. Thank you for the best days! Thanks for helping me to stay focused on something good. It gave me a feeling you could only get from true friends and family. I needed to be a part of that kind of love. Thanks for the support of my business and my family.

Rozz, thanks for your support, and for keeping me looking good with visits to Manifestation Salon. Thanks for letting me vent.

My "Ride or Die" girl, Marsha Hayes, you have seen it all the good, the bad, and the ugly. I have no words for the love you have always had for your baby sis. You could get my last! Thank you for praying and coming to my rescue when all hope was gone. You are truly a God sent friend. You don't talk, you act. I can never repay you for what you have done for us.

Thanks to my daughter, Nesey, and my god-children. Ya'll are "Fantastic" Thanks for the encouragement! Kesha we made it!

To my book helpers/supporters:
Thanks Angie for looking at it in the raw. Your feedback was helpful.
A special thanks to Niscey, my goddaughter, you went all the way! I'm not sure I would have made it without you.
Coach Laura, thanks for pulling me through until the end. You have done a great job with your SWAT leadership. You are a great leader!

Thank you, Melony. You are so awesome! I love you lil lady you have stuck like glue. I am so appreciative for the pictures, the front cover, the grammar check and the first look! Thank you for encouraging me to keep going… A giant THANK YOU!

My editor, Jessica D. Williams (Keen Vision Editing).Girl the enemy was chasing us from the start, but your prayers, perseverance and Godly wisdom is beyond your years! Your prayers proved to out run any attack. I'm glad to have you on my team. Jessica, I would not have finished without you. Thank you for believing in me. I thank God for you in my life. Another godchild and editor, look how blessed I am! Thank you, Jessica D. Williams. You Rock!

Last, but not least, my wonderful soulmate, Lemont Johnson. Your support was amazing! You have been a great, strong tower in my life. I call you, my gentle giant. Thanks for believing and pushing me to my destiny. I am so blessed to have found meaning and purpose in my life. THANKS, MY HONEY!

About the Author

Preheat the oven at 425 degrees. Mix one cup of ambition, two teaspoons of fun, three tablespoons of love, one cup of sass, and four cups of faith into a bowl. Beat it with heartache, pain, and abuse. Take a curvy pan and grease it with the love of Christ. Pour, bake, and have a slice of Renita Johnson.

The Bible story of the Samaritan woman at the well encompasses the life of Renita. "I was thirsty and broken," the author says. "It wasn't until I was quenched with the love of Christ that I was able to move past my pain, love others, and allow others to love me".

Her greatest joy in life is witnessing people overcome adversity and walk in purpose. Renita has lead several inspirational book clubs to help motivate others to seek God and uncover His will for their lives. In the future, Renita will host several seminars for abused women, just as she and her daughter, Kesha, planned before she passed away. "There are so many women battling hurt and pain," Renita says. "Those women need to know that life can and will get better. Even with Kesha gone, I must do it. I know this is what Kesha would have wanted."

Renita Johnson lives to inspire others through her stories of triumph and tribulation. The author is a Chattanooga, TN native who enjoys cooking alongside her husband, Lemont. The two run a catering service called LeMont's right in their hometown. Among her many accomplishments, she is a grandmother of eight beautiful girls and one handsome fellow, whom this book is written for. "A book never dies," the author says. "Even once I am long gone, my grandchildren will always have this book. They will always be able to read it and hear my voice. I pray that it lifts them up through any situation life may toss their way."

Contents

Acknowledgements/Dedication v
About the Author ix
Contents xi
Preface 1
1 The Blueprint 5
2 Damaged Goods 11
3 The Construction 17
4 Faulty Materials 23
5 The Addition 29
6 The Building of Love 33
7 Demolition 41
8 Cleaning Out the Attic 57
9 Making Sense of the Mess 63
10 Instruction Manuals and Warranties 69
11 Keepsakes and Treasures 73
How to Find the Treasures in Your Tragedy Workbook 77
Cleaning Out the Attic: The 30-Day Journal Challenge 79
    Day 1 81
    Day 2 83
    Day 3 85
    Day 4 87
    Day 5 89
    Day 6 91

Day 7	93
Day 8	95
Day 9	98
Day 10	101
Day 11	104
Day 12	106
Day 13	108
Day 14	110
Day 15	112
Day 16	114
Day 17	116
Day 18	118
Day 19	120
Day 20	122
Day 21	124
Day 22	127
Day 23	129
Day 24	131
Day 25	133
Day 26	135
Day 27	137
Day 28	139
Day 29	141
Day 30	143
Activity 1	145
Activity 2	146

Activity 3 147
Activity 4 148
Activity 5 149
Activity 6 150
Activity 7 151
Certificate of Completion 152
Certificate of Completion..149

Preface

You do not have to own an attic to understand its use. Even if you have never been in one, you have seen one. In scary movies, they serve as the perfect hiding spot for the 'boogie-man'. In other movies or shows, you may see children visiting an attic, uncovering family trinkets, grandmother's old clothes, or 'back in the day' shots of mom and dad. Attics are used for many different things, but the most common use for attics is storage. We use attics to store things we do not have space for in our homes. This is very similar to the way we use our mind and heart to store things we no longer have space for in our lives. Sometimes we pack our heartaches, abuse, and disappointments into boxes, seal them, and to further ensure their safety, we throw them into the back of our mind and the bottom of our heart. We feel that it is easier that way. We fail to realize that by securing their safety we endanger our lives.

I was raised in a time where you did not speak much about your emotions and feelings. "Leave well enough alone," they'd say. If something devastating happened, you dealt with it and moved on. Counseling was for the rich and the crazy. As a black woman, you just got through it. I cannot begin to tell you the danger in this old mindset. The most detrimental storage is stored pain. As time passes, we pile more and more on top of that stored pain. It becomes the roots of our mental trees of catastrophe, the roots of our hurt, and the roots of our pain. Depending on its nature, stored pain can lead to depression, obesity, anxiety, and several other mental and physical illnesses.

While some people simply store their pain in plain boxes, the rest of us try to cover our boxes. We attempt to make our boxes of stored pain look nice. We wrap our boxes of heartache, with nasty attitudes in an attempt to make everyone too afraid to get close enough to look inside. We wrap our boxes of doubt and disappointment with pride and rudeness, so that we never appear to be in need or without the answers. We wrap our boxes of insecurities with skimpy clothes, long weaves, and tons of make-up, hoping these things make up for the shortcomings of the gift lying inside. Unfortunately, covering stored pain is like using cheap wrapping paper. It gives a false security that the item wrapped is completely hidden. For the moment, it is, but with one wrong move, one wrong jolt, or one bad day the wrapping paper is ripped. Its contents are revealed. So what's in your attic? Are there boxes thrown everywhere, packed with the pain of yesterday? Are you afraid to open them, fearful of reliving every painstaking moment again? I've been there, and this is my story. I hope that through my transparency, you are able to begin your own journey of healing.

Time to Tell

You got a late start, yet there's so much to tell.
The hours are late.
Most of the pain and
many of the memories have faded away
But life has a way of unlocking the cage
and letting the butterfly free
There are many things I'm afraid to say,
But God has been very good to me
This journey has given me a few good licks
But the strength grew inside was worth the hits
Everything He allows is worth the pain
Once time stands still and we see what we've gained
My story is like a grape, mashed, bruised, and squashed
After being tossed to and fro in a basin to be washed
Life took what was left
Drained it into a bottle and placed it upon a shelf
Patiently a waiting for the right time or season to bloom
One day it's selected, opened, sampled, and consumed
Possessing a fine, smooth taste that's tangy and tart
With just enough sweetness to delight the heart.
Despite how long it's been caged
Life saves the best for last
Some things are just better with age.

Renita Johnson

The Attic

1 The Blueprint

Oh, the joys of growing up in the projects! I know what you are thinking, but in the 60's and 70's, the projects were a place where people raised their families with a sense of pride. The neighborhoods were safe and everyone treated each other like family. Parents did domestic work. Homes were always clean and well maintained. We had a small neighborhood store called Wheeler's Grocers. Wheeler's was the only store in walking distance, so we shopped there for everyday items. We also had our hang out-spot, Hamps. Hamps sold all types of treats and goodies; it even had a jukebox. After school, my friends and I would stop by to dance and hang out before we went home. Since my mother was so strict and over-protective, I had to rush home before she made it from work. You see, my mother was a single parent. Back then I never knew my parents were separated, as I grew up in a time in which children were not made privy to adult affairs. Though she was pretty tough, my mother taught me well. She did the best she could to raise five children alone. She insisted we did our chores and we did them without a grumble or very much allowance. Despite how hard she worked, she prepared meals of pinto beans and cornbread. We ate those meals at the table together every night.

School was great. Our teachers took pride in their appearance. They were great role models for me and my peers. It was so easy for them to teach in those days because it was understood that parents did not play about education. We went to school to learn, but the highlight of school for me was lunch! Our cafeteria served great soups and chili with butter on thick, toasted strips of bread, home-made rolls to die for, and grilled cheese sandwiches that literally melted on your tongue. Thursday was hamburger day. We were served delicious hamburgers with thick, freshly-baked cookies. Our holiday meals were truly something special, because those were the days my mom would always allow me and my siblings to purchase lunch at school.

I remember growing up in a family of love. We had family dinners together, slept together, played together, worshiped together, and of course, we fought together. We especially looked forward to each and every holiday! Christmas was exciting as a child. The presents would await us under our silver Christmas tree which was truly a sight to see! Our tree had a color wheel that shined upon the limbs of the tree, turning the tree red, then green, then blue, and finally yellow, over and over again. As children, my siblings and I would sit and marvel at that tree for hours. Easter brought new outfits and hairstyles for Sunday school, dyed Easter eggs, and home-made Easter baskets with jellybeans and hollowed chocolate rabbits. We would get colored, baby chicks that we named, chased, and fed for about three weeks before we petted them to death and gave them funerals consisting of a ceremony and proper burial! Summers were spent with Aunt Lavern. Boy was she a hoot! She was mean, the type of woman who did not mind cursing you out and going on her merry way. She loved me as much as I loved her, so I looked forward to spending every moment of my summer with her. She would take my cousin Nita and me to Taccoa, Georgia, a small country town outside of Atlanta. The train rides to Taccoa were so care-free and liberating! My cousin and I would stand right behind the conductor in the middle of the aisles. We sang and danced, entertaining every soul that could hear our voice. We were so excited about heading to the country where the air was clean, the food was fresh, and the animals ran untamed and free. Once we arrived to Taccoa, we had biscuits and gravy, fried chicken, fried potatoes, fresh greens, beans, yams, cornbread, and for dessert, cakes and pies of assorted flavors. The food was hallelujah good! Visions of those home-cooked meals are still vivid in my mind. Each year, without fail, I would eat so much that my stomach would ache and all I could do was lie on the couch and take Pepto-Bismol to settle my little stomach.

As my siblings and I grew older, I could see mom becoming more stressed. My brother was beginning his transition into becoming a teenager as my oldest sister transitioned from being a teenager to a teenage-mother. The stress of this caused my mother to change drastically. She began to show so much rage. She fussed and cursed all the time. My siblings and I began to fight like cats and dogs. A few of our fights even led to bloodshed. My mother's strictness had run its course, we just refused to follow her rules. Again, my parents were separated, so the toil and strain of this only made my mother's rage worsen by the day.

Once I started junior high school, I began to think about my future. I could not live in my mother's house forever. I was smart and a great leader. I began to think about someday leading my own company. In ninth grade, I wanted very much to be president of our student council. Despite the turmoil happening within my home, I worked very hard and was elected president. I remember how exciting that day was! After my win was announced, I went to the library to have my picture taken with Miss Tennessee and Mr. J.P. Franklin, our principal. The picture was placed in our local newspaper and my mother was so proud! In the midst of everything, my mother was still very serious about our education and our future. She wanted a different life for her children. I was determined to make her proud. Serving as president gave me hope. I felt I was looking at a bright future. As my junior high days

The Attic

ended, I began to plan for high school. Life was full of possibilities! I was empowered and ready to take on the world. Cheering with the cheer squad, singing in the choir, continuing drama class. The possibilities were endless! Little did I know, my care-free and optimistic life was about to take a turn for the absolute worse.

ENTATION WEEK: Miss Chattanooga, da Chubbs, center, was special guest participant during Orientation Week at Park Junior High School. The faculty dents presented a gift to Miss Chubbs cated an information handbook in left, are John P. Franklin, principal; DeNeese Fields, consultant of the Hou Libra Beauty Salon; Miss Renita C student council president, and Wal Johnson Jr., assistant director of th nooga Area Building Trades

Speak, My Child

Speak your story, my child. Speak until deaf ears are open.

Speak it until justice takes its place.

Speak your story, beautiful little girl

There are many like you hiding in this world.

Speak your story, strong little boys, Many, took the pain and continued playing with their toys.

The truths that are not told are stored in a box

Locked in all kinds of emotions.

Anger, fear, hopelessness, low self-esteem, hurt and distrust.

Someday, my child, you'll find the key to unlock that box.

Let the sadness explode. Let the fear escape

Let hopelessness bow down.

Let hope return to replace the pain

Let greatness come forth and your purpose be birthed.

Let trust sit on its throne and reign

Speak, my child, until your weary mind bends

with the peace of God.

Speak, my child, until the pain dies and is buried away.

Speak, my child, and allow happiness

to spring forth like a summer day.

Cry out, my child, until the darkness has melted away

And only the light of day has filled its space.

SPEAK, MY CHILD

Renita Johnson

2 Damaged Goods

My ninth grade year finally came to an end. Summer had arrived. I remember being so excited. This year, I spent my summer with my sister and her family. She and her husband needed a babysitter for my two nephews. Not only would I have the chance to make some money, but it was also an opportunity for me to breathe and finally be a teenager. My strict upbringing did not allow many chances for me to build friendships or be a care-free teenager. My sister and I had a great relationship. She understood my desire for a social life. Once I got a steady routine with my nephews, she allowed me to go out with my friends in the neighborhood. It was fun to play ball, have girl talks, look at boys, and do all the other things typical fourteen year-old girls did. Though I loved my mother dearly, living with my sister felt like I actually had one big happy family. My sister and her husband were like a mother and father to me. When my sister was off work, we would shop, laugh, talk, and enjoy each other's company. My brother-in-law watched out for me and treated me as if I was his own daughter. They provided the loving structure in my life that I had always desired.

"Nita," my sister called.

"Yes," I replied.

"What do you think about living here with us?" she asked. I mean, you're great with the boys and we could really use the help around the house.

"I would like that, I would like that a lot!" I exclaimed.

The Attic

I was on cloud nine! Living with my sister, going to high school, being free from my mother's tight hold, a fourteen year-old could not ask for much more! That night, after my sister left for work, I floated through the house. I fed my nephews their dinner, cleaned the kitchen, and put them to bed. I was exhausted, so I climbed into my bed myself. I laid there and just dreamt of what it would be like to live with my sister. I saw myself cheering my high school team to victory and waving to my family as they watched from the stands. I envisioned what it would be like to graduate from high school, walking across the stage, waving my diploma, and jumping for joy with my classmates. Life would be so awesome. I would go to college, start my own business, marry a nice man, start my own family – then suddenly I was awakened by a large mass of flesh. It laid atop my body and pressed into my chest like a ton of bricks. I could not breathe. My heart beat was so rapid it ranged out in my ears. A strong wind of alcohol swept across my face. The strength of the alcohol was so strong it burned my nose and stifled my already thin breathing. My body wanted to struggle to get free, but my mind was paralyzed with fear and confusion. A 200 plus pound, grown man was more than any fourteen year-old girl could manage to maneuver. I did not know what was happening to me. I felt his hands claw away at my panties and rip them off my legs. He roughly pried his lower body between my thighs. My thighs hurt from being forced to open, but it was nothing compared to what happened next. Flesh entered my small vaginal walls, and tore into them like a piercing hot iron. I screamed in agony and cried for help, but my sounds were muffled by the large hand covering my mouth. I struggled to suck in air between the grasp of his fingers. When it became too much to fight him off and fight for breath, I just laid there and gasped for air. I waited for the moment to end. Why was he doing this to me? I thought he loved me. He has been a father to me. Is this what fathers did to their daughters? Why did I so dearly want to have a father? Surely, I could have gone without this. My mind raced with so many thoughts as his thrusts became faster and harder. My small pelvic bone felt like it was being yanked out of my hip sockets. My vaginal felt like it had been surgically cut into strips. It burned so badly. "God, when would it all end?" I thought. Finally it did.

"Get up, quit crying. You need to go in the bathroom and clean yourself up," he mumbled.

He yanked me up by my arm, pulled me to the bathroom, and forced me to sit down on the toilet. Blood, urine, and semen streamed down my legs as snot and tears poured from my face. Did he think I wanted this? Is this what my life would be? What would my sister think? I held my head up to look him in his face. His back was turned to me. He prepared a hot vinegar douche. When he was done, he stuck a tube far into my already swollen vaginal. That feeling was absolutely horrible. The mixture of hot water and strong vinegar was more than I could bare. He left me alone in the bathroom. After I heard him collapse in his bed, I quickly mustered up enough strength to clean myself and the bathroom before my sister came home from work. Even once she got home, the smell of the vinegar was so strong in the bathroom and through the hall, I thought surely she would smell it and know what happened. But she never came in, she never said a word. What was I to do? How could I tell my sister? I would break up a happy home. My nephews would have to live like I did, without a father. What if my sister did not believe me? She would send me back home to live with my mother. Oh God! My mother and my brother! What if they found out? My mother would surely beat my sister to death for leaving me alone with him. My mother had always thought I was fast. She would always tell me my booty was too big to be prancing around grown men. Did I bring all of this to myself? In some way, had I beckoned him to rape me? I could not let my brother find out. My brother would kill him. My sister would be a widow, and my nephews wouldn't have a father. I tossed and turned through the night. I hated him for doing what he'd done to me. Why couldn't he have just left me alone? He ruined everything. I contemplated killing him, but I'd learned in Sunday school that God punishes us for doing wrong. My life was already a mess. The last thing I needed was God to be angry with me. My only option was to forget it ever happened. I would just go back to being a normal teenager. I would enjoy the rest of this summer with my friends, and maybe we could go back to being a happy family again. It was all on me. Everyone would be okay if I just shut up and forgot about it.

The weeks after the assault felt like years. I got out of bed every morning and tried to pull myself together enough to take care of the kids. The sight of my sister's husband made me sick to my stomach. My hatred for him grew stronger by the day. Whenever he would say anything to me I would glare at him, and respond with as much attitude as an abused fourteen year-old girl could muster without breaking down in tears. I would look at myself in the mirror each morning and be confused with what I saw. My body was different. I'd always been curvy for my age, but I'd never paid much attention to it. I would spin around a few times, to look at my butt. I could hear my mother's voice ringing in my ears.

"Nita, sit your fast tail down somewhere, doing all that dancing." she'd say.

"I love dancing," I thought to myself.

Each morning when I looked in the mirror, I began to hate myself. I once loved the way my breasts sat up, much more fuller and perkier than most girls my age. I once loved my waist line, how it was so small and perfect. No matter what I wore, I would look so cute in it. My butt was nice and round, like a ball. I remembered how my friends would admire my body; they wished they did not have to use tissue to fill their bras and underwear. Every single thing I once loved about myself felt dirty. Each night I went to bed prepared and ready for him to burst through the doors again, but he never came. I figured he'd forgotten about it. So I tried to forget about it too.

After a while, I began to go back outside to play with my friends. I ran around, played games, and just tried my best to forget about everything that happened but the memories just kept playing back over and over again. I only had a few weeks left before school started back. I really wanted to enjoy this time. One day, I was running around with my girlfriends when a guy approached me.

"What are ya'll doing?" he asked.

"Minding our own business!" I responded.

"What's your name?" he said with a smile.

"Who wants to know?" I snapped!

"I do," he said.

I looked at him and said "Renita."

"Hey, Renita." He replied, still smiling.

"Hey." I tried to be as mean as I could, but he was so cute, I could not help but smile.

My friends ran off in a fit of giggles. He and I sat and talked for so long that day. I loved being around him. For those last few weeks, he became the highlight of my summer. I looked forward to the days when my sister was off work, just so I could get outside and talk to him. We had great conversations. He was so nice to me. He asked if I would be His girlfriend. I said yes with a great big smile. We kissed a few times and when things began to get serious, we had a conversations about sex. One night we did have sex. I was so emotionally disturbed, it was horrible. The only thing I could think about was my sister's husband and the attack. My boyfriend did not understand what happened and I definitely did not tell him.

3 The Construction

Weeks later, I missed my period. I was terrified at the thought of having to tell my sister. I knew she would be so disappointed in me. Even though she got pregnant in high school, she wanted so much more for me. I thought back on how she was so proud of me whenever I got Honor Roll or any other honors at school. My sister thought so highly of me. She constantly encouraged me to go to college. How was I going to go to college with a baby? So many thoughts ran through my mind.

Finally, one Saturday morning, I built up the courage to tell her.

"Can I talk to you?" I asked as she was making breakfast for my nephews.

"What do you want, Nita?" I'm trying to get breakfast made for the boys so we –

"I missed my period."

"You what?" she exclaimed.

"My period, it has not come this month." I mumbled.

"That's what you get! Running around here with that little boy all times of the night. You done messed around! I knew y'all been doing something! Didn't I tell you to just worry about school? Now you done got yourself pregnant! How are you gonna take care of a child? How is he gone help you? You know that little nappy-head boy ain't got no money to help you do nothing with a child!" She ranted.

The Attic

I just stared at her. I wanted to tell her how her husband came in, in the middle of the night and took my virginity. I wanted so badly to tell my sister the truth, but I stood there silent as she went on and on. Eventually, I walked away and left her fussing. Later on that day, I heard her on the phone. She said something about taking me to the doctor. She had a friend whose mother was a nurse. My sister took me to her house. The lady asked me to sit on the bed.

"Hey baby, how are you doing?" She asked.

"I'm okay." I grumbled.

"Well your sister said you done got yourself in a little bit of trouble, so we are gonna see if we can help you out. Pull your panties down and lean over a little. I'm going to give you a shot. This is gonna hurt just a little. After you leave today, I want you to tell your sister if you see anything in your panties. It may be just a little blood, or it may be a lot, but whatever you see make sure you let her know. Understand?"

"Yes ma'am." I said.

The next few days I felt a little weird. I threw up a few times. Each time, my sister ranted and raved about how fast I was and how this baby was going to teach me a lesson I'd never forget. I did not see any blood until almost two weeks later. It was a brownish color, and a small amount. I did not tell anyone. I did not want a baby, but I definitely did not want to abort one either.

One evening, I overheard my sister on the phone. I sat in my room with my ears pressed to the wall to hear as much of the conversation as I could.

"She ain't seen nothing."

"Naw, and if she has, she ain't said nothing yet."

"She may just be too far along already."

"She might just be."

That was it. It was all over. As I packed my bags to go home, tears flooded my face. Every dream, every hope, and every bit of joy I had about living with my sister was gone. Before she took me home, my sister took me to the doctor's office to confirm the pregnancy.

I remember peeing in a cup, taking all of my clothes off, and putting on a white, paper cover. I laid on top of the cold table as I waited for the doctor to come in. Once he came in, he lifted up the white paper that covered my nakedness.

He looked at my breast and began to touch them in a massaging way. He rubbed both of my nipples at the same time in a circular motion. In my mind, I knew that something was not right. I was very afraid and confused. I thought that he was supposed to touch one breast at a time. He looked at me with a smile.

"How does this feel?" he asked in a very soft tone.

I never responded. I looked away at the wall. My mind was all mixed up. I'd just been raped and now this doctor was rubbing on my breast. I laid there in deep thought until the exam was over. Will I always be mistreated by men? Had I become a target? What was really going on? Once the exam was over, the doctor left the room. He left me lying on the table feeling worthless. After the door shut, I jumped down from the cold table and dressed as fast as I could. I ran out of the room and told my sister I was ready to leave. The doctor spoke with her and confirmed what I feared most. I was pregnant. Fourteen years old and confused.

The Attic

I moved back home with my mother just as the summer ended. School had just started back again. My dwindled excitement about being in high school was completely incinerated the moment my name, along with a few other girls, was called to the front office. Back in those days, pregnant girls could not go to regular high schools. We were sent a few miles away to another school for expecting girls and other women. The four of us walked to the bus stop in shame each morning. It wasn't like now-a-days how teenagers and unwed women are proud of their pregnancies. We did not flaunt our bellies with cute maternity clothes. We wore oversized clothes or a tight girdle to hide them for as long as we could. Older women sitting outside and on buses, looked at us, and shook their heads. We were ridiculed and talked about worse than a dog. We kept walking with our chins pressed heavily into our chests. We hated being known as the 'fast ass, young girls who could not keep their panties on', but we knew better than to respond.

My pregnancy felt like it lasted forever. The months went by slowly. One evening, I wobbled in from school feeling horrible. My body ached and my stomach felt as if something was writhing within, trying to get loose. I laid down for a while, but it did not help. I went to the bathroom and realized there was pink show in my panties. I hobbled downstairs in pain. My mother immediately took me to the hospital. When I arrived at the hospital, I laid on the table. Wow, I thought. This is really happening to me. I'm having a baby. The birthing was easy, far easier than the conception. In fact, the pain from the rape made me numb to everything that came after.

I remember the first time I laid eyes on my beautiful baby girl. I gave her the name, Kesha. Unlike most mothers, I did not gaze upon her with loving eyes. I was emotionless as she squirmed around in my arms. As I watched her, visions of that dreadful summer night flashed before my eyes. As I stared at her face, she looked just like me, I was relieved. I thought, maybe she does belong to my boyfriend. I prayed she did, but only time would tell.

4 Faulty Materials

My boyfriend and I decided we would try our best to raise Kesha together. Back in those days, 'shacking up' was out of the question! My mother took us to Ringgold, Georgia where we were married. We lived with my mother. She helped us to raise Kesha as I finished high school. I spent the rest of my teenage years angry and hurt with a root of bitterness so deep I did not even like myself. In high school, I was either the class clown or the one fighting and cursing out other girls. Although it was rough, I still tried to be a normal high school student. I hung out whenever my mom allowed me and agreed to babysit. I even went to prom.

After I graduated high school, things with my husband and I came to an end. We slowly drifted apart. By that summer, we were divorced. My relationship with my mom worsened as well. I was a grown woman, but I felt like my mother still wanted to treat me like a child. I was so tired of the constant fussing and fighting, so when Kesha was five I let her live with my mother while I stayed with a friend and got my life together.

I got my first real job at T.C. Thompson Children's Hospital. When I began to work as a nurse assistant, I met two fascinating women, whom I affectionately called Miss. T and Miss. V. Miss. T and Miss. V kept me in line. We were all single women. We made a pact amongst ourselves and a few other young ladies to be accountability partners. We vowed that we wouldn't have sex until we were married. None of them knew about my Mr. Man. I kept that to myself. You see, Mr. Man and I met when I was a nursing assistant student. Even though we had a bit of an age difference, we were attracted to each other. At the beginning, Mr. Man and I just talked on the phone, nothing serious. I knew early on that Mr. Man was the player type. My talks with Miss. T and Miss. V kept me from doing much with him. As Valentine's Day approached, the ladies and I got serious about our pact. We felt lonesome around that time. On Valentine's Day, we sat and talked before we left. We discussed our plans and everyone was spending Valentine's Day alone, except me. Of course I did not tell the ladies my plans. I knew they would try to talk me out of them. I wasn't having that at all. Mr. Man and I had planned to hang out that night. Once I got off of work, I ran home and got everything cleaned up. I put on a cute, little outfit and sprayed my perfumes. A few hours later, Mr. Man walked in the door with a nice bottle of wine. At first, everything was okay. We drank, laughed, talked, and enjoyed some music. It was all good until the effects of the wine kicked in. Suddenly, we were in the mix!

Over the weekend, all I could think about was admitting to the ladies that Mr. Man and I had sex. I made up my mind that I wasn't going to tell them jack! I would keep my secret to myself for as long as I could. I spent the rest of my Valentine's weekend in bed. For some reason, I'd started to feel sick and tired. I went to work that Monday and just plopped in a chair.

"Uh, hey, Renita," Miss. T said.

"Hey," I replied.

"What did you do this weekend? You look all tired, "she said.

"I ain't done nothing," I snapped!

"Oh, okay then. Well what's wrong with you? Why are you over there looking like that?" she asked.

"I'm fine. Ain't nothing wrong with me," I replied.

So as the ladies came in, they all boasted and chatted about their good weekend and how they kept their word and did not have sex. I remember sitting, looking stupid, hoping no one would ask me anything. Even if they did, I wasn't feeling well, so I was ready to get them out of my business real quick.

A few weeks went by and I noticed I'd missed my period. "Damn!" I thought, "Not again."

I took a home pregnancy test and it was positive. How in the world can I keep this from Ms. T and Ms. V? I knew I could not, so the next day at work I pulled Ms. T to the side.

"Miss. T, I need to talk to you, just you by yourself," I snapped!

"Why? What's wrong, Renita?" she asked.

We went into the lounge, away from everyone else. I wasn't quite ready for everyone to know my business. I was so disappointed in myself.

"I'm just gone flat out tell you, and I don't care what you think about me," I started.

"What, Renita? What is it?" she asked.

"I done messed up! I'm pregnant!" I cried.

"What? How did that happen? With who?" she questioned.

"Hell I don't know! We used everything spermicide, condoms, ain't nothing worked," I exclaimed.

"When did this happen?" she asked.

"Valentine's. I knew we wasn't supposed to be doing nothing, but it did not start out like that. He brought some wine. That was it," I admitted.

By this point, I was crying so hard, she could not make out what I was saying. She promised not to tell anyone until I was ready.

Slowly but surely, everyone began to put the pieces together. My already horrible attitude had gotten off the chain. I was lazy. There were times when I would just lay down on the couches in our lounge area and do absolutely nothing. I was nauseous. My tolerance level was so bad, people could not say anything to me without getting their heads bit off. I snapped at everyone. Coworkers had it hard dealing with me. It did not matter. In addition to this, I'd started to gain weight. When I was about five months, a young lady on the third floor decided she would mention how fat I'd gotten.

"Dang Renita you lookin' a lil' thick 'round the middle. I guess you done got yourself pregnant," she said in a snooty way.

Well that was it. I cursed that girl out so bad someone called our supervisor and told her there was ruckus going on in the cafeteria. Shortly after, I was called to the office. Once I got there, I just sat and tried my best to play tough.

"Now, Renita, what happened? You were reported using profanity and attempting to fight another assistant," she said.

"I ain't got nothing to say," I snapped!

"Well, let me put it to you like this. I've heard that you were pregnant. So you know like I know that you need this job. We're gonna put you on probation. I feel like you just need a few days at home to relax and get yourself together," my supervisor said.

I did not go to work for three days. When I returned, everyone knew I was pregnant. They looked out for me and steered clear of me at the same time. Everyone except Miss. T and Miss. V. They did not play with me. Despite how mean I was, they kept telling me the truth. They loved on me through it all. It was something about those women. They just knew how to handle me.

Since the baby was due in November, I took my maternity leave in October. My last day at work was a tough one. My coworkers said they wanted to plan a baby shower for me, but my attitude had been so horrible they decided not to do anything for me. I could not believe it. My feelings were hurt. I may have been mean, but I supported every baby shower for every other girl. So on my last day, I decided to confront my coworkers about their decision.

"Miss. T," I started. "Let me tell you something. If you think I care that ya'll ain't throwing me a baby shower, I don't. I don't need none of ya'll. It's just gone be me and my baby anyway. I don't care what ya'll do or say about me. I have everything I need". I replied.

"Okay Renita," she replied.

I was pissed. How dare she talk so calmly to me? It was almost like she just did not care. So with my hurt feelings and all, I did my last rounds and checked the vitals of my patients. Just as I was beginning to clean up, I was paged to the lounge.

"What the hell?" I thought.

You see, the floors were a long way from the lounge. By this point, I was eight months pregnant. I heaved and rolled myself and my belly to the lounge, cursing the whole time. When I opened the door to the lounge, all I heard was "Surprise!"

I looked around the room. I was so confused. There were baby decorations hanging from the ceiling. A beautiful cake and other finger foods sat on a nicely decorated table. There were presents lined against the wall, on the table, everywhere! Tears begun to flow down my face. "They actually do love me," I thought to myself.

The ladies and I laughed and talked for a while. Miss. V helped me get everything to my apartment. I'd gotten so many nice gifts. As a single mother, I felt very blessed. I'd gotten everything I needed to welcome my baby into the world.

Miss. T and Miss. V took good care of me during the last few weeks of my pregnancy. They would call, make house visits, go with me to the doctor, and help me run errands. Through the week, I'd rest and enjoy visits from some other close friends. On Fridays, Kesha and I would go to Aunt Laverne's and spend time with her, Nita and De-De. Aunt Laverne would fry fish and I'd sit there and eat. On Sundays, I sang in the choir at church. Our choir director, Ms. Janice, had taken me under her wing. She was a great mother figure during that period of my life. After church, I'd go home with her family. Each Sunday, I'd sit on the couch with my feet propped as she prepared Sunday dinners. They took very good care of me.

Mr. Man and I had not spoken in a while. When I told him I was pregnant, he had just found out that the woman he'd been seeing was pregnant as well. He already had other children, so he made it clear that he did not want anything to do with my child. The support of my Aunt, stepmom and friends helped to fill that void tremendously.

5 The Addition

It was a brisk November morning. I had been up most of the night tossing and turning with pain. For some reason, I still woke up early. I took Kesha to the bus stop, hobbled back in the house, and laid down for a while. Around 9 a.m., the pain had not subsided, so I called Miss V we knew it was probably time to have the baby. She told me to time the pain, and call her once the times began to get close. So I did. I took a bath, packed my hospital bags, and made arrangements for Kesha. When the contractions were five minutes apart, Miss. V came over to pick me up. We packed everything in the car. Once we got to her house, we began walking. We walked up and down a hill several times. I fussed and cursed every step of the way, but Miss. V just kept on pushing me. Finally, I felt like I had to pass a bowel movement. We rushed to the hospital. Once the doctor finally got there, I was already in full-blown labor. It was too late to get an epidural or any pain medication so the doctor gave me a small shot in my vaginal to numb the pain.

"Help me!! Somebody help me!" I shouted.

"Somebody get her quiet," the doctor said.

"Honey, you wasn't doing all that hollering when you made this baby. Now hush all that fuss. It's time to push this baby out!" the nurse snapped!

"You can shut the hell up! You don't know what I was doing when I got pregnant," I snapped back!

"Now look, it's not gonna be any of that," the doctor said. "It's time to have this baby."

Around 12:45, the doctor checked me and announced that the baby was crowning. I yelled and squirmed around on that table like I was dying. They strapped me down, placed my legs in the stirrup, and dropped the bottom of the table. My legs were shaking like a fan. I squirmed around so bad I tensed my butt. This kept the baby from coming out. Would you believe that nurse climbed on top of my stomach, I mean right between the bridge of my breast and stomach and started to push? I screamed so loud people in the waiting room could hear me. Finally, a fat little baby girl weighing seven pounds and four ounces came out of me.

"Tie my tubes! Tie my tubes right damn now!" I shouted.

"No ma'am. We have to wait 24 hours until we can do that," the doctor replied.

"Oh no you ain't either. You gone tie my tubes and you gone do it right now!" I screamed at him.

"Renita, you're losing a lot of blood already," he snapped!

"I don't care! I'm about to die anyway. I'm not ever going through this again. Tie my tubes!" I yelled.

The doctor looked at me for a moment, then told the nurses to prep me for surgery. He went to work stitching the tears in my vaginal. I felt every pierce of that surgical needle. Afterwards, they gave me a long pad and some hospital panties. What happened next was more than I could bare. I got a little 'laughing gas', but it did nothing to numb the pain of that knife slicing between the bottom of my stomach and my navel. I started to yell and the nurse threw something over my face. When I woke up, I was in the recovery room and there was a baby on top of my stomach.

Kesha, Miss. V, and Miss. T helped me to take care of Nesey after I returned from the hospital. I stayed at home for about a year before returning to work.

6 The Building of Love

Who me? Yes, me! I know it may seem hard to believe, but love found me! So check this out. By this point, I had been working at the Children's Hospital in central supply for almost 8 years. I told myself, "Renita, it's time to get it together, honey! You need to focus on your career and your life!" I'd gained so much weight dealing with the depression of being a single mother. I tried so many different diet pills and weight-loss programs, but nothing worked. Right when I thought the weight was off for good the numbers on the scale crept right back up! I started to live by my scale. If the numbers were low, I was okay, but whenever those numbers got high again, I was depressed. I really hated my life. I just could not get a grip. So one day, in the midst of everything I had going on, I got a call from my youngest sister on my mom's side.

"Nita, I got somebody I want you to meet." she said.

"If it's a man, I am not interested," I replied.

"Here she goes", I thought. "Why is she trying to hook me up? She knows good and well that I don't have time for a man".

"But girl, he so nice, I just think ya'll would be great together," she said.

"No ma'am," I snapped!

"He has a cute little boy," she went on. "You know you like little boys, he is so adorable. You will love him. I cannot wait for you to see him. I'm gonna bring him by."

Since I had a few days off work, she brought him over to my house to play with the girls. My sister was right. He was the cutest little curly-headed fellow you'd ever want to see. He had an adorable country accent. His name was Lemonta. We enjoyed having him at the house.

My sister called. I knew she was up to something. She told me that Lemonta's daddy wanted his son and needed to know who I was. That sneaky little devil, I thought. Nevertheless, I agreed to speak to Lemonta's father.

"This is Renita," I said plainly.

"Hey Renita how are you?" he asked.

"I'm fine," I replied.

"Well, I've heard a lot about you. I cannot wait to meet you," he said.

"We'll see. One day. Maybe," I replied.

He was a nice man, but I was still bitter. I wasn't ready to let a man in my life again. He did not have any transportation, so I felt safe. I could keep him at a distance for as long as I wanted. We began to converse more and more. I was shocked! I really enjoyed our conversations. I was a talker and he was a great listener. I guess he realized I had no plans of meeting him any time soon. So he took matters into his own hands and asked if we could meet. I was hesitant, but I agreed to stop by his house after I got off work.

I did not know what was about to happen! All my life, I'd been taught to always look my best, so I made sure I was looking real cute! I had on my red pants and a little cute shirt. Once I got there, he came outside. I just looked at him. He stood about 5'8". He may have been about 125 pounds – soaking wet. He was slim! He had a full head of hair that had been combed straight to the back with very little style. He was different from any man I'd ever dated. I mean, of course, I'd be a good catch for him. I was a young girl, thick in the right places, and easy on the eyes. I had a job, an apartment, a car. I was smart, direct, and very witty. He was homeless. He had just moved in with his friends. In those days, older women taught us that if a man did not have anything to give you, you did not have a single thing to give him – not even your time. What in the world was I to do with this man? He was nice and all, but I definitely needed more convincing before I made a decision. At that point, I wasn't sure about our chemistry or our future together.

After our first meeting, we continued to talk over the phone. I slowly started to let my guard down and allowed him to meet my girls. Crazy, right? Lemonta loved to come to our house. Our children felt like we were one big, happy family. Wait a minute, I thought. Nesey ran around calling him daddy, and Kesha just wouldn't shut up about how much she wanted him to be their dad. As for me, well, I just wasn't sure. I did not know how I would let this man into my heart. This meant nothing to him. Lemont proposed to me that November. I felt like we were moving too fast. I was numb, happy, afraid, and bitter all at the same time. The next

July, we had a big, happy wedding. Lemont even cooked all the food. I never realized how great of a chef he was until our wedding day. Would you believe even though everything was so beautiful, I was still searching for the negative? I constantly waited for my happily ever after to come to a tragic end. I still did not get it. What is he really here for? When is he going to leave? Why did he want to get married and care for me anyway? Those thoughts constantly roamed my mind. I realized I could not love him for real. I kept asking God why I could not feel the love Lemont had for me? Why couldn't I love him the way he loved me? I did not realize that it wasn't just Lemont I could not feel love from anyone. It was time to  allow the love of Jesus to start the healing process in my heart. The time had come for me to learn how to trust the God in people. I truly believe that my husband, Lemont, was designed just for me. It took a strong soldier to take the punches and keep standing. He did just that. No one else could have loved me through all the hell I'd taken him through. God trusted him with all of my injuries and he loved me until they disappeared. Lemont was the master key God used to unlock the mess and bitterness locked away inside of me. I remember nights when my husband would minister to me. He truly allowed God to use him to free me. If it was not for the hell he chose to endure, I wouldn't have the freedom to write today. My husband understood my purpose, even when I did not. He spoke life into me and never left my side. Lemont encouraged me to be all that I could be, and most importantly, to be in God's will. I was able to see God through Lemont's eyes of love. Lemont is proof that soulmates really do exist.

LOVE FOUND ME

I could not believe I was so blessed

To encounter God's love on Earth.

Battered, bruised, and ripped apart,

Nothing seemed to penetrate my heart.

My Knight in tattered armor,

He too had been battered by the storms of life.

We were introduced to each other by the

forced winds, rain, and the angry strands of life's hardest times.

Our hearts begin to intertwine our thoughts, trust, and beliefs.

When agreed we could weather them together,

It truthfully blew my mind.

A sign of hope and laughter started to break through,

This felt like enough to last forever.

On one knee, on a cold November night, my Knight promised

too be committed to me for the rest of his life.

My hand he held as he stared into my eyes.

My heart was penetrated when he stated

I was all he ever looked for in a mate.

Because of his love, I've became one of the

Richest women on this earth that was my fate.

To find a soulmate is one of the best blessings

God can do to restore your heart.

Most people receive it, but because of the work involved,

They quit before time and the season start.

A quitter will never ever win and a winner will never ever quit.

We promised to hold up our vows

And keep them in the path of righteousness.

When one of us gave up, the other one held them up before the King on the throne.

Somehow it just kept lasting,

I guess the key is we're singing our same song.

Serve each other like you're a king and queen

Don't forget to say and do the same great things.

When love is found and nurtured, these things it brings;

Friendship, Time, partnership, A soulmate you will see

*I'm so glad that **"LOVE FOUND ME"**.*

7 Demolition

The rape caused me to be bitter because I knew I could never tell a soul. How could I put into words what happened to me when I was fourteen years old? Who would believe me? Besides, who would even care? When it came to Kesha, the secret of the rape made me feel dishonest and distant. She did not have a true identity of her roots. The man she thought was her father, was not. I worried about what would happen to her if I never told her the truth. How would she respond if she found out on her own? The guilt and shame kept my lips sealed. I never wanted anyone to know my weakness or feel sorry for me, so I tried to appear tough as nails. I was a mean woman. I was rude to people and did not care two things about it. Family members and friends would talk about how tough I was on Kesha. They often ridiculed me for treating her as if she was the one who got pregnant at 14 years of age. As a teenager, Kesha often complained of how over-protective I was. I did not allow Kesha to date or have sleepovers. I wouldn't have been able to live with myself if the same thing happened to either of my daughters. As a result, I was as strict and mean as my own mother.

After she graduated high school, Kesha went straight to college. Since I kept her caged up at home, she was wild and crazy once she got there. She lost her scholarship and returned home. We argued all the time. Kesha decided to join the military. She went to California and was one of the smartest soldiers they had. She tested so high that her sergeant wanted her to enroll in officer school. Before she got her permanent duty station, she met her future husband, got pregnant, came back home in her fifth month, and had her first (of three) daughters. After that, Kesha lived all

The Attic

over the world. She loved to travel. She never met a stranger. She lived in Chattanooga TN off and on. As she got older, Kesha and I began to talk daily. We slowly began to re-build our relationship.

When Kesha was about 36, something happened that changed our lives forever. I remember the day like it was yesterday. I sat around patiently waiting for her to call me. The phone finally rang. It was Kesha.

"Mama," she sobbed hysterically.

"Baby, what's wrong? What did the doctor say?" I replied frantically.

"It's breast cancer. He said it's not looking too good." She cried. "The ultrasound is showing that it's in stage four."

My heart dropped. I had been on pins and needles all day waiting on Kesha's call. Two weeks earlier, Kesha's breasts had begun to leak. She self-examined herself and found a lump in one of her breasts. We immediately called the doctor to schedule an appointment. A mammogram and ultrasound confirmed what we had feared. It was breast cancer.

In the beginning, we called each other every day in tears. It was so hard to believe that my daughter had cancer. I instantly thought back to that horrible summer when I was fourteen. I still hated my sister's husband for what he'd done. It just wasn't fair. I could not understand why (almost 36 years later) the rape was still tormenting my life. That tragedy was still causing me to feel so much pain. Since Kesha father died with cancer, I always worried that the same thing would happen to her.

Kesha began chemotherapy. Months passed, however, there was still no progress. The radiation from the chemo had burned her entire chest. It was so painful to watch my daughter lie in a hospital bed with her chest oozing with blisters. Her hands and feet had turned black. The medication caused her to have tongue and throat sores that would last for weeks. Her hair had even begun to fall out, so she decided to cut it all off. "I'd rather cut it off than to have cancer take it off," she would say. Her strength was amazing. Despite the illness, she was still the diva we all knew and loved. She would fix her make-up and make sure her jewelry was always on point. She rocked the hell out of that bald head! I'd never seen anyone look so sexy and beautiful with a bald head.

It appeared that she was getting better. The reports showed no signs of cancer. We were hopeful. Her husband had gotten an assignment in Washington State, so she was finally well enough to make the move. I was so nervous about her moving and being so far away. We were very afraid that the cancer would rear its ugly head again.

Six months later, she called complaining about her hip. I told her that it was probably just from standing on her feet all day. I asked her had she seen a doctor; of course she had not. Half way through her shift she called me. Kesha was in so much pain that she left work to go to the emergency room. I was at work finishing up cakes and orders for pick up in our Bakery kitchen. It was right before the Christmas holiday and we were very busy. She called back and told me the doctors had done x-rays and it looked like just a small hip fracture. I was relieved, but only for a short while.

A few moments later, Kesha called back.

"My bones have spots all over them. The stage 4 breast cancer is back. There's nothing they can do for me. It's that fatal, mama." she cried.

I tried my best to console her screams and cries. I could not breathe. My entire nervous system was shattered. I cried all day. My first customer came for her pick up.

"Renita, I came for my coconut cake! Renita? My God, what's wrong?" she asked.

"It's Kesha," I cried. "It's over for her. She's gonna die. I don't know what to do. This is not fair. She is too young. What about her girls? What are they gonna do without their mama. This just ain't right."

"Renita, can we pray?" she asked.

I never responded. She took my snot and tear covered hands and prayed. That pain was greater than any I'd ever felt. As she prayed, I begged God not to take my daughter. I begged Him to heal her and forgive me for my hatefulness. I thought about all the years I spent resenting Kesha for being the product of rape. All the time I spent wishing, praying, and hoping that I wasn't pregnant, and that I wouldn't bring a child into this world. But I did bring her into this world. Now she was leaving it. It was all my fault.

Early spring of 2011 approached. I was so worried because Kesha had stopped calling me with reports. In fact, she never wanted to talk about it. She chatted about the girls and how things were going with her and her husband, but no matter how upbeat she sounded, I felt the pain in her voice.

I met a guy one evening at a dinner party. There was something in his eyes that made me feel safe. We began to share our life stories. He told me how his mother died from cancer a few years ago. I immediately began to shed a few tears. I told him about Kesha dying from cancer and being so far away from our family during this tough time.

"I got a bonus from work, and I'd been wondering why God had sent this unexpected blessing," he began. "Now, I know why."

"Why," I asked.

"I'm going to purchase plane tickets for your daughter and her three children. She needs to be here with her family as soon as possible."

My mouth dropped. I could not believe God had sent this angel to us. He looked online and ordered the four tickets. Miraculously, the cost of the tickets came to the amount of his bonus.

When my family and I went to the airport to pick up Kesha, I searched frantically for her. When I saw her, I ran to her. She was in a wheelchair, looking like a DIVA!

"Well, look at this queen on her throne!" I exclaimed. We all laughed. We tried our very best to make the occasion a happy one. Though we could see the weariness in her eyes, we smiled at our beautiful warrior.

We decided to give Kesha a surprise birthday celebration. Her husband whisked her away on her first cruise so we could plan. Over 200 guests showed up to celebrate with her. She was so happy! It was the most beautiful party I'd ever done. Everything was decorated in pink, grey, and silver, with lights everywhere.

"Well, baby, did you enjoy your birthday?" I asked Kesha.

The Attic

"Mama the party was beautiful! I'm so grateful to have so many people who love me. The cruise was so nice. We had a real good time! When I die, you have to promise me that"

"Kesha, shut up!"

"But Mama..."

"Kesha, no!"

"Mama."

"Baby..."

"It don't get no better for me on this side of heaven, mama," she sighed.

By this point I was in tears. Kesha looked better than I'd seen her in months. I'd never heard her speak of death so calmly. It was almost as if she was welcoming it. I could not bear the thought of my daughter leaving. It was still a very hard pill to swallow. But on this warm summer day, she explained to me that she was ready. She went on and on about how she had created a bucket list, but I really could not hear anything she said. My mind went back to another summer night, years ago. How on that night, I experienced the death of my childhood and her conception, and on this night I was actually discussing the death of my child that was born out of the pain of my childhood. This was so far from what I thought my life would be. It had to be a God to keep me sane.

By September 2011, things started to get real. Kesha decided not to continue chemotherapy. It only made her sick. One Friday evening, she came home about 5 or 6 from Disney World. It was the last thing on her bucket list. The family and the hospice nurse checked on her that night. Things weren't looking too good. When I made it home to her, she did not even look me in the eyes. It was as if she was looking at something; something earthly eyes could never see. I returned to work that night to prep. We had committed to serving over 250 people at a local church the next day. Morning came. Kesha did not rest well that night. The doctor was called. He stated that it was best the hospice cared for her; she was no longer responded to us. We did not know her needs anymore. Hospice arrived around one that afternoon to take Kesha to the hospice center. I remember watching as they placed her on a stretcher in a sitting position. I walked up to the stretcher, held her hand, kissed her, and said "Bye, Kesha."

After everyone left, I locked up. I got in the shower and cried. I knew it was time to release her to the Lord, but I just wasn't ready yet. I got out of the shower, dressed, and left for work. Lemont and I prepared to serve the 250 people as promised, but we planned to leave as soon as we were done to be with Kesha in her last moments. I arrived at work and started to help with the meal preparation before it was time to serve.

It was almost 3:30 p.m. when I heard my phone ring.

"Hello." I answered.

"She's gone…Kesha just died…she is gone."

"No, no, not yet! I needed her to wait! I told her I was coming up there. She cannot be gone."

It was Kesha's husband. His voice was so shaky and broken. Our entire family was devastated. Lemont broke down in tears. He decided to stay and finish serving the 250 people. I called a few friends to assist him while I left to see Kesha. I sadly drove alone

The Attic

to the hospice center. Kesha's entire life began to play in my mind. I began to hear her voice, as a teenager.

"Why don't you love me?!" she cried.

"I do love you, I had you didn't I?" I snapped back.

"Mama, I did not ask to be here. You messed up!"

"I did not ask for you to be here, it wasn't my fault that you are here."

I remember rolling my eyes and walking away from her. She was just a teenager back then. A little girl in my eyes. She was so irritated with me and my over-protective ways. I remember her complaining about not being able to date, go to parties, and have sleepovers. As a mother who had been raped at an early age, I just could not fathom the same thing happening to my daughter. She was so frustrated, and so was I. I never told her the truth because I felt like she was just too young to understand. So in retaliation, I was mean to her whenever she questioned my mothering tactics. When Kesha got older, she reminded me of those days. She never forgot how I made her feel in those moments. Now my baby was gone.

I regretted those moments when I looked at her and became sick to my stomach. As she matured, she looked more and more like her father. Each time I looked at her, it reminded me of the pain. It was so hard to watch; as his face suddenly became part of hers. I was, remembering how nervous around family gatherings I would be, waiting for someone to say how much Kesha looked like her male cousins, which we really her brothers. I remembered the day I finally told Kesha what happened. I told her that I was raped by my sister's husband. I told her that he was her biological father. We both cried for hours. She told me how sorry she was for what I had been through. I assured her how much I still loved her.

Kesha had such a good heart. Even in the midst of her sickness, she refused to die with things being the way they were. Before she died, she told the man that she had been raised to believe was her biological father the truth. We visited his home and she told him I was rape and that he was not her father. She told him that she needed closure before she died and she wanted her mother's life to have peace about how she was born. She hugged him and told him "No more lies. I need to rest in peace, no matter how anybody else felt, I will leave this earth knowing my mom was free of the bondage that weighted her down all her life". Kesha said. "My mom is now free to tell our story, to help other to break free of their past". He replied, "I don't care. I gave you my name, I wasn't in your life, but you will always be my first born. I love you Kesha!" She even made peace with all of our family members.

My load was just beginning to lighten, and now Kesha's gone. I was so confused with God. Why now? Why my baby? Why did she die the same way as her biological father died? Cancer snatch her life! Why am I suffering? It wasn't my fault! Is this fair? Why me God? WHO ARE YOU? You're the God of love? Did you say you love me? How do you expect me to trust you now? I was so angry and hurt.

When I finally made it to Kesha's body, I was numb all over. The process was over, whatever she needed to do was done. It was finished. I never felt so sick, hurt, and overwhelmed. Would I ever move forward after this? I thought. My first born, my special love child had vanished off the face of the earth leaving me only a smiling shell to look at, to kiss, and to lay on. I remember opening her eyes once I got there to see if any life was left in those pupils for me to wave a final good bye. I now remember, after 3 years, that I said my final goodbye as they lifted her into the stretcher. It was in that moment she said her final goodbye to me.

EdKesha LaShon Scott
May 26, 1972 - October 22, 2011
Olivet Baptist Church
11:00 a.m., October 28, 2011
William McKinley Holloway, Jr. Officiating

Mom,   9/25/08
         midnight

Thank you for opening up your house to me and my family. I know we have had some rough times, but God always see us through. This diagnosis was a wake up call for our whole family. I want nothing more than to see us healthy in all areas..... emotionally, spiritual, & ~~mental~~, body. I feel that this is our time to get it right. Something is going on in our family and only God will finish it. If you have prayed and fasted and believe that this surgery is the answer, than God will see you through.

I love You!
Your the best Mom Ever!

P.S. What is your love language? I'm trying something.   Time / Service / Touch / Gifts / Words

Renita Johnson

5/30/11

Mom & Dad

Thanks so much for the love and support you have shown me & my family over the past few months. The party was just the icing on the cake. You guys just always keep going above and beyond the call of duty. I can't say "thank you" enough! Your selflessness is only due to your love for God! I appreciate how you have stepped up to take care of my children and know that if anything happens to me, I know that you both have got our backs! I love you guys so much for all that you do! A "thank you" card is not enough but it is the only way to get the point across!

The Attic

January 19, 2011

Mom,

Thank you for being there for me whenever I need you. This is going to be the most difficult test of our relationship yet. I pray that we become closer than ever through this situation. I'm so glad that you decided to carry me for 9 months and give me life. It would have been may easier to abort me or give me up for adoption. Although it was a difficult decision thank you for making it. Please don't continue to blame for this misfortunate turn of events. We both must forgive him and move on. You was so on the mark when you said that God didn't owe us anything and that in everything we should give him Praise. We should continue to praise him so that the "Wall" will come down! (will receive my healing)!

Thank you for opening your home for me and my family. Please know that I'm so gratefully for what you are willing to do for me and my family. May you be blessed with many more days of God's grace! I love you!

Love, Keshia Scott

My Voice

I'm glad to share my voice with the world

I have a voice that needs to be heard

I have a voice that has meaning

My voice has healing

My voice has something to share

There's history in my voice, there's peace in my voice

There is always a story to tell. It brings clarity to many souls

It brings love to a lonely heart.

It brings redemption to a weary start.

It has brought joy at the top of sorrow.

There is always hope inside tomorrow.

My voice is original, yet the stories may be the same.

Somehow the victims change.

I'm glad to share my voice with the world

Give your pain to the healer. He can bear it all - the guilt, the shame, the fear

Someone needs to hear your story.

It's worth it all because God gets the glory

I'm glad to share my voice with the world

Renita Johnson

8 Cleaning Out the Attic

Your mind is very similar to an attic. First, let's dig into the basics of an attic. Merriam-Webster defines an attic as a place or space under the roof of a house, typically used for storage. Attics are often neglected, rarely cleaned or straightened out. They are oddly shaped and have several hard-to-reach nooks and crannies. Attics also play a huge role in the temperature of a house. Attics account for nearly 15% of energy loss, even in the most updated of homes. In elementary school, you may have learned that hot air rises. As a result, for homes with attics, hot air is trapped and it is retained. This produces extreme moisture, creating a perfect environment for mold. Mold in an attic is detrimental to the rest of the home because it causes decay in the structure of the attic, ultimately weakening the structure of the entire home.

Oddly Shaped

Since attics are normally the space between the ceiling and the roof of the house, they are oddly shaped. This can make using the attic for anything other than storage very difficult. In some attics, there are areas where you can stand up completely, whereas in other areas, you may have to duck down to dodge rafters or roofing. These same areas exist in the minds of people who have been abused. When you have been abused, your mentality is disfigured in such a way you find difficulty using the full capacity of your mind in every circumstance. People who have been abused may be able to think great when it comes to work or their career. However, in the areas of family, personal relationships, and friendships they tend to "duck down" to dodge those that attempt to get close. The shape of an attic makes certain spots difficult to reach, and hard to clean. Abuse creates these same unreachable and dirty places in our minds. We refuse to think about it because it hurts too much. Abuse is defined as improperly or wrongly using something. When we are treated improperly, we in return treat ourselves improperly. Abuse of any type leads to a lowered self-esteem because anything that does not lift you to your rightful place in Christ, tears you down. Most victims of abuse question their own value because someone else treated them as if they were worthless. Having low self-esteem leads to the neglect of our health and our well-being. Abuse inflicted upon us by others sometimes leads to self-inflicted abuse. We try to avoid everything that reminds us of those abusive moments. We honestly believe that this helps us, but as we discussed earlier, stored pain can cost us our lives.

Neglected Storage, Negative Storage

In the preface, we discussed how stored pain is boxed and stored in your mind. Your mind holds memories of things that have taken place within your life. The good memories are great to store and save. They remind you of the great things you have accomplished, the love you have felt, or the good times you have had. The bad memories have the potential to wipe away every positive thought a good memory brings. Have you ever been having an awesome day, then suddenly one bad thing happens and ruins everything? This is a horrible habit that many of us have, but it is a clear view of how our minds have been conditioned to work. Within your mind lies thoughts and situations from birth to wherever you are now. When you focus too much on the bad things that have happened in your life, you blur out everything else. You make yourself believe that your life has just been one rough ride, when in actuality, it's been a great ride with a few rough bumps. Think about an attic. We may have some really awesome things stored up there, but we can never get to it because of all the junk around it. Because our attics are so jumbled and junky, we cannot see the good things it stores.

ATTIC "Anything Trapped That I Control"

What's in your attic? Is there anything in your attic that you have trapped, but are willing to remove? Personally, my attic once represented a mind full of bad memories and thoughts of yesterday. I was paralyzed with fear and pain. I could not move forward. I held on to the bitterness and heartache of those who hurt me. Ten years ago, I was diagnosed with a medical term called, Sick Sinus Syndrome. Today, I have a pacemaker placed in my heart. During my regular visits, my cardiologist reminds me to live as stress free as I can.

We were not designed to carry the weight of the world on our shoulders. Philippians 4:8 says "Finally brothers and sisters, whatever is true, whatever is noble, whatever is right, whatever is pure, whatever is lovely, whatever is admirable—if anything is excellent or praiseworthy, think about these things." When we spend time thinking upon everything that has gone wrong, we neglect what has gone right. We neglect every happy moment that taught us how to smile. We neglect every moment that taught us how to love. We even neglect ourselves. A person who has been raped once physically has been raped almost a thousand times more mentally. Why? Because they replay the moment over and over in their mind. Each time they replay the situation in their mind, they abuse their mindset.

Mental Mold

The effects of rape or any abuse can cause serious physical and psychological trauma. The physical wounds are easy to treat, but the emotional scars, though they are less visible, are the hardest to treat. The emotional effects of rape can last for years. Abuse causes a range of emotions that continuously weave in and out of our minds. We often ask ourselves questions like, "Why did this happen to me?" and, "What did I do to deserve this?" These questions haunt us when we sleep at night. They cause us to question every good thing that happens to us, and every loving person that comes our way. Abuse causes us to wonder when everything will come crashing down again.

Check out these different emotions and the turmoil they cause in the minds of the abused.

Confusion: *Why me? Why now? What have I done to deserve this? What do I do now? Who do I tell? Who can I talk to? Will they believe me? Can they help me?*

Self-Doubt: *No one will ever love me again. I'm not good enough. I'm damaged goods. I'm dirty. Everyone knows. They can see it all over my face.*

Anger: *I hate them for doing this to me. I want to kill them. I hope something bad as this happens to them one day. I hope they pay for this.*

Embarrassment: *I hope no one ever finds out. People will look at me funny. They will treat me like I'm dirty. I feel so dirty.*

Distrust: *Do my friends and family really love me? Are they really here for me? Should I give dating a chance? Will they find reason to abuse me? Who's next?*

Denial: *Nothing happened. It's all in my head. I made it all up. I'm fine.*

Guilt: *It is all my fault. I brought this on myself. I got exactly what I deserve. I made them think that was what I wanted. I sent the wrong signals. I only have myself to blame.*

Lack of Faith in God: *Why did God allow this to happen to me? I thought He was a protector. Is God even real? What have I been believing in? How can He love me? What kind of person can truly love the whole world? God cannot be real, because He allowed this to happen to me.*

The Lord, our God, is not the author of confusion, therefore our minds were not designed to have so many different emotions at once. We refuse to let anyone hear our cries, we refuse to allow anyone else to help us through our pain. When we allow our minds to have so many emotions at once we become overwhelmed. Just as with anything being pushed to its limits, we overheat. When we allow ourselves to overheat with emotions, we create an environment in our mind that is suitable for the growth of mental mold. Mental mold is just as devastating as physical mold. They both are detrimental to the structure. Physical mold destroys a home. Mental mold destroys a body.

Mental mold...

*Wakes you up in the middle of the night in sweats.

*Makes you eat when you are not hungry.

*Causes you to mistreat everyone you meet the way you were mistreated by others years ago.

*Tells you to hate yourself, your life, and everything around you.

*Causes you to operate outside the will of God.

*Holds your dreams and aspirations hostage.

*Ruins you and your Family too.

Mental mold causes the decay of your entire mind structure. If the structure of your mind is decaying, so will the structure of your entire body. Think about this. What are you allowing to be retained in your mind? What are you allowing to cause decay and weaken the structure of your mind and body?

9 Making Sense of the Mess

The majority of things that happen in our lives never make sense, but they make up life. When you try to make sense of the mess, you attempt to get common knowledge out of a situation. Why did it occur? What lesson should be learned? How can this be avoided? The sense we make of our messes depend solely upon our perception, the understanding we pull from situations based upon what we believe and what we want to see. The mind is an amazing thing. There have been several studies on the mind and all its wonders. Our minds perceive life in two ways: sensory and extra-sensory. Making sense of messy situations require an extra-sensory approach. An abused and cluttered mind cannot make sense of a mess, because it does not have the space or opportunity to use what it uses on a daily basis to get through life, the five senses. Think about the five senses for a moment. They allow us to get an understanding of everything around us. We can see the sky and know if it is day or night. We are able to smell things and figure out what they are. We hear sounds and are able to decipher from where or whom they came. We feel things to know if they are hard or soft. We taste food and within seconds know if we will ever try it again. Extra-sensory goes way beyond what we see with our eyes, hear with our ears, feel with our physical bodies, taste with our tongues, or smell with our noses. Just as we use the five senses to gain knowledge of the world around us, we use our five senses to gain knowledge and understanding of the things that have taken place in our lives. So the first step in making sense of the mess, is getting in touch with those five senses on an extra-sensory level.

Feeling: After being abused, the sense of feeling is usually the first one we try to dismiss. We think that if we train our minds not to feel anything, we will be okay. Avoiding our feelings and not dealing with them seems like the easiest and best thing to do. If we are numb to those feelings, we will not feel the sting of the pain. What we fail to realize is in avoiding pain, we subconsciously begin to avoid any other feelings that we think will someday lead to pain. This includes love, peace, happiness, and joy.

This is the worst way to deal with abuse. Pain is not always a bad thing. Pain alerts you that something is wrong. If you are able to feel pain, you can pinpoint where it hurts and what treatment is needed to make it go away. In a sense, pain tells the brain where to apply the pressure in order to stop the bleeding. Find someone to talk to and acknowledge how you feel. The sooner you can face those feelings, the sooner you can get rid of them. Packing them away affects every other aspect in your life.

When we are abused, instead of embracing love and happiness in relationships and friendships, we constantly worry about being hurt by people who proclaim to love us. As a result, we ruin our families, friendships, and relationships by being distant and cold. We do not allow people to get too close in fear that they will bring us sorrow, or find something bad enough about us to make them stop loving us.

Understand that people will hurt you, some knowingly and some unknowingly. People will find out things about you. There will be things they like and things they will not, but to someone who really loves you, it will not matter. You may have disagreements, but this does not mean they will hurt you or abuse you the same way someone else did. Pray for discernment, and give people a chance. Give your family a chance. Deal with your feelings so that you can live a life of happiness and joy with those that love you. They did not abuse you, and they do not deserve to be abused by you.

Hearing: People who have been abused tell themselves a number of things to get through the day. I am convinced that when you speak, hear, or say anything enough, you eventually begin to believe it. This is why hearing is a very important sense. Anything negative creates blockage and keeps you from hearing the words that could set you free. The Word of God tells us that faith comes by hearing. So what do you hear? Blockage does not only come from within. Our surroundings play a huge part in what we hear and do not hear. Most of today's music and media create blockages by degrading our people and glorifying drugs, fornication, and violence. Because of the internal struggle to remain positive, victims of abuse should refrain from this type of blockage. Become surrounded with positive music and positive people that will speak life into you when you are at your lowest. Put notes on your mirror, and recite them to yourself as you prepare for your day. Allow God to speak to your heart and mind through daily devotion and quiet time.

Taste: The sense to taste is wonderful. Unlike the sense of feeling, people run to the sense of taste to heal their problems. Satisfying our taste buds takes our minds off the situations temporarily. Slowly, but surely, we become addicted to a method of indulgent healing. When dealing with abuse, we must be careful about the things we choose to indulge. Most addictions cause obesity and other health issues. When you are addicted to something, you constantly seek the feeling of euphoria it creates. We naturally gravitate towards anything that gives peace, especially when we are in a state of confusion. Food, drugs, alcohol, sex, and other things of that nature only help you temporarily. After the last chip, the last hit, or the last drop, the effect eventually wears off. We find that we are left with the same feelings we had before we indulged. Develop a taste for more effective methods of dealing with abuse. Develop a taste for the word of God, positive interactions with family and loved ones, meditation, and counseling. These activities are more effective in the healing process.

Smell: The sense of taste and smell are linked. We can usually tell how something tastes because of the smell it gives off. Smelling allows us to taste things without completely indulging them. Some animals, like snakes, even use their tongues to smell because they are without noses. For this reason, just as you watch your addictions, you should watch your attractions. One of the first ways we become attracted is through smell. We are able to smell food and decide if we want it without ever seeing it. It is amazing how our noses and sense of smell work.

By nature, we are attracted to things that are familiar or comfortable. The question is, what have you become comfortable with? Have you become comfortable with abuse? Do you suddenly seek abuse in your relationships? Have you allowed yourself to become the victim in every situation? Some women who experience some type of abuse become attracted to abusive men. Depending on the time spent in an abusive relationship, they begin to expect abuse in every aspect of their lives. Have you become so familiar with abuse, that you expect it? Do you seem to always find yourself in abusive situations? If so, it is time to check your attractions. Have you become drawn to situations and people that hurt you? It is impossible to make sense of a mess if you have become attracted to the aroma of your afflictions.

Seeing: Seeing is a sense afforded to us by our eyes. The eye is made of many parts, several of which can teach us a lesson or two about spiritual sight in our life.

Sclera- Responsible for flexibility and strength. Despite how much we map out our lives, we can never plan for the heartache and abuse. Flexibility allows us to be open to the unplanned occurrences that life throws at us. Being flexible means even though we do not accept the confusion, we understand that it may occur.

The cornea- Houses tears which maintain oxygen exchange and water content. There are times in life where we sometimes forget to breathe and let things out. As we discussed earlier, abuse has the potential to shut you up. We refuse to cry because we do not want people to realize that we are hurting. Whenever you get something in your eyes, the cornea releases tears to rid the eye of anything that causes pain or stops the eye from doing its job. Becoming a victim of abuse is very similar to getting dust in your eye. Let the tears flow. Tears are a sign of release and renewal. Allow your spiritual eye to formulate tears to wash away anything that is blocking or altering your spiritual sight.

Anterior & Posterior Chambers- Maintains the shape of the eye and proper spacing of the elements we see. Learn to separate things. Your past is just that, your past. It belongs behind you. So quit blending it with your present and your future. Your head is not positioned to turn around completely, neither are your eyes in the back of your head. We were created on purpose. Do not isolate from others because of fear of how they may hurt you. Your sight is very important in making sense of the mess. Do not allow abuse to skew your vision and keep you bound.

10 Instruction Manuals and Warranties

In every attic or place of storage, we can find instruction manuals and warranties. These are usually strewn about in our mess with everything else, but in order to make sense of a mess we will need to locate these items.

Instruction Manuals
Imagine buying something new, cutting open the box in excitement and pouring all the pieces out on the floor. Once you realize everything you have, you may get confused on how to put it all together. The last thing we look for is the instruction manual. We try our best to piece everything together on our own. At first, our little project seems to be fine. It appears to be functioning well, but after a while, it begins to fall apart because it was not properly put together. Life is a lot like this. Sometimes situations and circumstances are dumped on us. We try to handle it, but we get so overwhelmed with trying to put the pieces together on our own. This creates a bigger mess than we had before.

An instruction manual is a booklet designed to tell a buyer everything they need to know about their purchase. An instruction manual provides us with information on…

- Safety instructions
- Assembly Instructions
- Usage instructions
- Maintenance Instructions
- Warranty Instructions

We are going to deal with each portion of an instruction manual and its importance.

Safety Instructions: It is important that we know the safety precautions for anything we decide to deal with. Something's have the potential to hurt us. There are some lessons in life we do not have to learn through experience. There are people around us that have experienced certain things so that we do not have to. In reading the safety instructions we seek the wisdom we need to avoid stupid mistakes. If we listen to the wisdom around us, we do not have to fall as hard on our own behinds.

Assembly Instructions: Just as we mentioned before, sometimes life just throws things at us. We do not know how to put them together unless we read the assembly instructions. Assembly for our lives can be found by seeking God. We should seek him for guidance and understanding when life does not quite make sense.

Usage Instructions: Everything in life happens for a reason. Sometimes we use situations that occur in our lives as crutches. We allow pain and hurt to be an excuse for mistreating other people. The Bible tells us that no weapon formed against us will prosper. They will form, but they will not kill us. With this being said, the things that happen to us happen for us. Instead of being depressed about difficult situations, push through and seek the lesson it teaches.

Maintenance Instructions: How well we maintain our belongings determines how long they will last, and how long they will perform proficiently. This is the same way with our minds and hearts. We must take good care of them. If we are careful about how we maintain our hearts and minds they will serve us better.

An instruction manual aides us as we attempt to use things the way they were designed to be used. The Word of God, the Bible is the ultimate instruction manual. It tells stories about different people, the mistakes they have made, and how they sought God. Thanks to the Bible, we do not have to go through trials by fire, but in the event that we do, the Bible also provides guidance on how we can get through those things. Do not wait until after you see the assembly fall apart to use the instruction manual. Use it before! When life throws you so many different pieces, don't get overwhelmed or try to figure it all out on your own. Search the Bible for guidance. If you do not have clear direction on where you are going, it will make it difficult to get there.

Warranty Instruction: Have you ever bought something and in less than two months it stopped working? Most items come with a warranty, while others require you to purchase a warranty. If you have a warranty, you can send the item back for troubleshooting or replacement of the item altogether. Sometimes, even when we have read the instruction manual, and used the item properly it still manages to malfunction. Warranties are great to have because some things can only be fixed by the manufacture.

The warranty we have on our lives works the same way. Even after we have gone to God for help, things do not always go as planned. His love warrants us to be able to come back to him no matter how many times we malfunction. Our warranty is purchased and redeemed by our faith. Warranties are important to keep up with. Sometimes after we have purchased a warranty, we place it in our attics or in a junk draw. We do not look for them again until our item has malfunctioned. This may be a fine way to handle our earthly warranties, but this is not the way to handle our spiritual warranties. We should remind ourselves of the warranty we have through Christ daily. Daily walks with him keeps our warranties close in sight should we ever need it.

11 Keepsakes and Treasures

One of the hardest tasks of cleaning is deciding what to keep and what to throw away. After making sense of a messy situation, we must review it and decide what memories to keep and what memories to dismiss. Was this meant to be in my life for a reason, season, or lifetime? Most of the mess in our attic accumulates from things we just do not want to get rid of. Each time you rediscover your keepsake, it brings a greater desire to hold on to the memory. In our attics, we store things we know we will never use again, but the strain of cleaning it is so much, we tend to just leave things the way they are. So let's take a moment and go through our boxes.

I remember in an old box, I had an old purse. It had keys on an old key ring. We did not have a clue what the keys unlocked. We thought they started one of our old cars or trucks, we stuck it back in the cluttered bag knowing we did not possess either vehicle anymore. So why did we stuff the old keys back into the bag? We were afraid that we would someday need them. Those keys reminded me of anger. We had them, but we did not know what they would unlock. In life, we will encounter many situations that fit our empty slots of pain. They line up perfectly in the holes in our soul. This is a time that causes us to respond with a negative reaction. These soul-keys may come in the form of a person or situation. You do not need them, but they fit so perfectly, because the pain is not healed. You must reset the lock in your heart and discard the keys. To reset means to heal. Once you are healed, the combination changes automatically. The old keys do not control or unlock anything in you anymore. Remember, healing is a process. Now let's focus on how to decide if something is a keepsake or if it is really a treasure.

Take a look at the thoughts that are occupying your mind. Are they keepsakes or treasures? Keepsakes are usually little trinkets you get from baby showers, weddings, graduations, and other celebrations. They are designed to help you remember the special occasion and events. Such as, my children's birthday, graduation days, my wedding day, my first cruise, Baby's first tooth, first step, and even the closing of my dream home.

Treasures are a little different. Treasures are rarely given away. Most treasures are discovered. The most beautiful treasures I have discovered are Kesha's memories. Whereas keepsakes depreciate in value, treasures grow in worth daily. Keepsakes remind you of what happened. Treasures define the value of what happened. Sometimes they are realized through hard work and determination. Great treasures are chosen.

There are several keepsakes I had to dismiss. I had to stop reliving the turmoil, the images of the violent rape I encountered, the constant desire to stuff my face to remove the pain, constant anger, rage, guilt and shame. All these keepsakes will clutter your mental attic and keep you from living a life of peace and destiny. The treasure, however, lies in the lesson that the situation has taught me. Examples of my treasures are: The life I gave Kesha, the choices to love and care for her and my entire family, the strength that has come though pain, the 39 years of Kesha's memories, the three granddaughters she gave me, the healing power in Jesus' garment, the treasure of leaving a legacy of this book for my grandchildren, and of course, the treasure of my soul mate. These are only a few treasures I will share. There are so many more. I also treasure the fact that through all my adversity, pain, suffering, abuse, rape, shame, being misunderstood, and definitely, the guilt that stays with you like a twin sister, my thoughts are that my grandchildren and readers will press through life's challenges and pull great treasures from your life to remind you to live with purpose no matter what. Once you realize the difference between a treasure and a keepsake, and are willing to accept the challenge, you will be able to thoroughly clean and organize your attic. Let's review, renew, and restore your life. You are worth the work!

RENITA'S TREASURES

How to Find the Treasures in Your Tragedy Workbook

The next exercises are designed to interactively help you in cleaning out the attic. Prayerfully upon the completion of this workbook, you will be able to:

- Pinpoint negative situations and occurrences that you have stored mentally.
- Realize how these negative situations are affecting you physically, spiritually, and emotionally.
- Seek Christ and release the pain.
- Clean your attic and keep it clean.

The exercises are designed to help you apply different tactics to clean your attic and keep it clean. When completing the assignments, open up and be honest with yourself. This is the only way you will ever truly heal.

Cleaning Out the Attic: The 30-Day Journal Challenge

Writing is known as being therapy for the soul. It allows you to pour out your heart without saying a word. Writing is especially helpful to those who are not ready to verbally express the trauma they have experienced. Even if you have not experienced some type of trauma, you will still benefit from this attic clean-up. It only takes 20 - 30 minutes per day! Designate a quiet place where it is only you and God.

This journaling activity is broken into three portions.

Day 1 - Day 10 - *Dealing with the Hurt*

Day 11 - Day 20 - *Getting to Know You, Again*

Day 21 - Day 30 - *Dreams, Goals, Aspirations, and Desires*

Motivate yourself every day to get through this challenge. If you miss a day (which I know you will not) just pick up where you left off! Keep pushing! Your life depends on it! I'm excited! Let's get to work!

DEALING WITH THE HURT

For the first ten days of our journaling, we will focus on pulling everything out of the attic. We will keep what we need and throw away the rest. Don't hold back! Open up and get that junk out of there! You may not be strong enough to tell the world how you feel just yet, but you could, at least, be honest with yourself. You will never be able to get through the pain if you never admit to yourself that you are hurting. Do not numb yourself. Be real with yourself.

Day 1

Write about a traumatic situation you have dealt with in your life. When did it happened? How did it make you feel? How has it changed your life? Who knows? Why haven't you told anyone? These are just a few questions to get your writing going, but feel free to write whatever you want!

MEDITATION

Give yourself a pat on the back! I'm sure it took a lot to open up and relive those moments, but you have just taken the first step to cleaning out the attic. I'm proud of you!

Day 2

Think about your entire life. Have you done something that you are not proud to admit? Does it still haunt your mind? Have you owned up to it? If so, what was the outcome? Were you pleased with the outcome? If you have not owned up to it, what's stopping you?

MEDITATION

Most of our stored pain comes from what has been done to us. However, there are also something's that we have done and feel guilty about. No one is perfect. We all fall short of God's glory. If you have not owned up to it, call the person or try your best to make amends. It is never too late. If you are unable to talk to the person directly, spend some time in meditation with God. Confess to him what you have done wrong and accept His forgiveness.

Day 3

"Dear Past, Me"

Write a letter to the "you of the past". What lessons have you learned that you wish you knew back then? What would you say to the old you?

MEDITATION

Let's admit it, we have done some crazy things in our lives! Some situations happened out of our control, while others we could have avoided. We cannot go back in time and change our mistakes. At this point in our lives, we can only be thankful for the lessons those situations taught us and try our best not to repeat those same mistakes again. This letter serves as a reminder that there has been growth our lives. As long as we have breath in our bodies, we have a chance to get it right if we are open to growth!

Day 4

What grudges are you currently holding? What keeps you from releasing those grudges?

MEDITATION

It is crazy how we hold grudges about the smallest things. Holding on to grudges can make you bitter. Take some time and re-evaluate the grudges that you are holding. What would it take for you to release those grudges? Now that we are discussing them, are they even worth holding?

Day 5

Enough is enough! Forgiveness is not a favor you do for other people, it helps you more than it helps anyone else. So, who do you need to forgive? Make a list of the people you need to forgive.

MEDITATION

Letting go of those grudges require forgiveness. Just as we would want someone to forgive our wrongs, other people deserve that too. We measure our wrongs by the amount of pain they cause, but in the eyesight of God, all sin is on the same playing field. Forgive those that have hurt you. Right your wrongs. Let those grudges go. Meditate on forgiveness. Build up the courage to call or visit those you need to make amends. You will feel much better, and your spirit will feel much lighter.

Day 6

How do you deal with anger and other emotions? What do you do to calm yourself down and get a grip?

MEDITATION

After reading my story, I'm sure you saw some of the ways I chose to deal with anger. All bad! When we are angry, we sometimes say or do things that we regret later on. Review the ways you deal with anger. If you deal with anger through addictions, pray to be released. Find other ways to deal with anger. Exercising, writing, developing hobbies, and spending time alone are just a few ways you can redirect the negative energy that comes with anger and other negative emotions.

Day 7

We have all had those "should've, could've, would've" moments. These missed opportunities tend to weigh heavily on our hearts and our minds. Write about some opportunities that you may have missed. How do you think your life would be different if you had taken advantage of those opportunities?

_____
_____
_____
_____
_____
_____
_____
_____
_____
_____
_____
_____
_____
_____
_____
_____

MEDITATION

Our regrets keep us up at night. Whether it was marrying the love of your life, going to college, taking your dream job, or visiting a loved one before they died, we all have regrets and moments we wish we'd done things differently. It is time to face the music. We can never get those moments back. Everything happens the way it does for a reason. Though we may not be able to pinpoint why we missed those moments right now, everything will make sense as we continue to move through life. Do not focus on the opportunities missed. Look forward to the opportunities to come!

Day 8

What are you worried about? It can be something as small as getting the shower fixed or something as big as finding out who's the father of your child! Whatever it is, write it down.

The Attic

_____
_____
_____
_____
_____
_____
_____
_____
_____
_____
_____
_____
_____
_____
_____
_____
_____
_____

MEDITATION Review your list. What can you do about it right now? If it is a bill, do you have the money? Do you know how you could get the money? If you answered no to any of these questions, worrying about it will not make the money magically appear. If your worries can be taken care of right now, today, this minute, then go do it! But if it is something you can only do tomorrow, or later on, you are wasting time and effort worrying about it right now. Worry is the trick of the enemy. Worrying gets you so worked up about things you have no control over, that you do not have the strength or brain power to think about the things you do have control over. So today, say goodbye to worrying! Anytime you begin to worrying about something ask yourself three questions: Can I do something about it right now? How soon can I fix it? What could I be doing right now?

Day 9

Today, you are going to make two lists. First, make a list of things you would never want to lose. Think about keepsakes and valuables that mean a lot to you. The list can be as long as you like!

Renita Johnson

Now, imagine that your house is being flooded. You are given a bag to preserve only five valuable things. Make a list of those things!

1.
2.
3.
4.
5.

MEDITATION

We hold on to so much, most of which we do not need. This is why there is so much clutter in our attics. In the first part of our writing exercise, you made a list of things you could never part with, but you found in the second part that you actually could live without those things. It is amazing how we can get rid of things when we are forced to do so. The heartache, grudges and regrets we hold onto can damage our health. Before you are forced to make a decision between your health and your stored pain, let the stored pain go.

Day 10

Are you ready to let that thing go? Well let's do it. Write a letter to one person you need to forgive. Imagine that you are face to face with them. Let it all out! Remember, this letter is personal, so do not be ashamed to really let your emotions out!

MEDITATION

Did that not feel good? You have gotten it all out. This letter serves as your mental eviction notice for them and the emotions they brought about. They have been evicted and they cannot come back! It is time to live your life without anxiety or fear.

GETTING TO KNOW YOU, AGAIN!

Congratulations! You made it through the first ten days of attic cleaning! Take a look around your attic. Can you finally see a path? Can you finally see the good things you have hidden? Well let's focus on those things! Over the next ten days, you will be reminded of who you are, and reveal what you may have never known.

Day 11

Create a list of people that helped you along the way. How would your life be different without them?

MEDITATION

You may have had some people to really hurt you, but you have also had some people who helped you and spoke life into you when you were at your lowest. If at all possible, contact them. Let them know how much they helped you. Let them know how much you appreciate their impact on your life. Let them know about the journey to healing you have decided to take. Allow them to motivate and encourage you to keep on pushing!

Day 12

How was your day? Really! How was your day? What did you eat for breakfast? What errands did you run? Who did you see? Write about your day from when you awoke to this very moment.

_____
_____
_____
_____
_____
_____
_____
_____
_____
_____
_____
_____
_____
_____
_____
_____
_____
_____
_____
_____
_____

MEDITATION

We live life at such a fast pace that we sometimes forget to take a step back and look at everything. How you spend your day is a true reflection of who you are and what you feel is important. Every night, before you go to bed, take some time and think about your day. What could you have done more of, what could you have done less of? How do you feel about how you spent your day?

Day 13

Who are you? Describe yourself without saying your name. If you met someone for the first time, what would you tell them about you? What defines you? What do you believe in? What matters most? What has life taught you? What is your God-given purpose?

_____
_____
_____
_____
_____
_____
_____
_____
_____
_____
_____
_____
_____
_____
_____
_____
_____
_____
_____
_____
_____
_____
_____

MEDITATION

If you know who you are, nothing negative can happen and define who you are. Knowledge of self helps us to heal to heal and prevent pain. Despite how the enemy tries to tear you down with self-doubt or self-pity, continuously remind yourself of who you are!

Day 14

Think back to a happy moment. Where were you? What happened? Who was there? What made this moment so special to you?

_____
_____
_____
_____
_____
_____
_____
_____
_____
_____
_____
_____
_____
_____
_____
_____
_____
_____
_____
_____
_____
_____
_____
_____
_____

_____

MEDITATION

When we experience trauma in our lives, we tend to forget about all the great things that have happened to us. Spend some time thinking about other happy moments. Keep these moments fresh in your mind. Refer to them whenever you get discouraged about life.

Day 15

Think back over your life, even back to your childhood. List all of your accomplishments. Spend some time tooting your own horn!

MEDITATION

In addition to taking away happiness, abuse has a way of making us feel as though we have not gotten very far in life. You have done some pretty awesome things! Acknowledge them, even those accomplishments you have not made private. Self-pride is very important in the healing process.

Day 16

Before you begin writing, go look in the mirror. What do you see? What do you love most about what you see?

MEDITATION

Do you see what I see? I see someone beautiful, gorgeous, & handsome! What do you love most about yourself? It does not matter if anyone else thinks the same, what do you think about you?

Day 17

What do you like? List your five favorite places to visit, 5 favorite foods, 5 favorite things to do, 5 favorite people to spend time with.

MEDITATION

In knowing yourself, knowing what you like is very important. Review your list. Think about why you like these things. Treat yourself to some of your favorites when you are feeling down. Whether it is taking a trip, calling one of your friends to chat, or preparing your favorite meal after a rough day, spending time doing what you like to do is a very important part of cleaning your attic. It helps you to decipher between the things you were given and the things you actually enjoy. Take control of your life! Enjoy yourself.

Day 18

What do you think defines a person?

MEDITATION

Review what you believe defines a person. Compare it to what you wrote about yourself. How well do you meet your definition? What are your strengths and weaknesses? Think of a few ways that you could improve yourself.

_____
_____
_____
_____
_____
_____
_____
_____
_____
_____
_____
_____
_____
_____
_____
_____
_____
_____
_____

Renita Johnson

Day 19

Yesterday, you wrote about what defines a person. You meditated on ways that you could improve yourself. Write those ways. Be sure to include how you will work towards your personal self-improvement goals.

MEDITATION

No one is perfect, but we can spend each day working towards becoming a better person. If you would like to be better groomed, more knowledgeable of certain topics, happier, or whatever it is you desire to improve in your life, it all starts with you! How will you begin today?

Day 20

Write a letter to the future you. What questions would you ask yourself? What would you remind yourself? Feel free to say whatever you would like!

_____
_____
_____
_____
_____
_____
_____
_____
_____
_____
_____
_____
_____
_____
_____
_____
_____
_____
_____
_____

MEDITATION

The past is behind you. The future is yours for the taking! This letter will motivate you to become the person you want to be! You can read this letter three months or three years from now. It is totally up to you! Hide the letter in the back of a closet you need to clean and read it once you accomplish your goal. Mail the letter to a friend and ask them not to open it until you come for a visit. Be creative! You will be surprised at how you feel once you have accomplished your self-improvement goals!

HAVE FAITH, LIVE OUT YOUR DREAMS, AND ASPIRE TO BE GREAT

Well, look at you! You have made it through 20 days of attic cleaning! This is such a big accomplishment! You should be very proud of yourself. I know I am! Abuse and trauma has a way of suffocating our dreams, hopes, goals, and aspirations. It binds the faith we have in ourselves. It is time to look our fears and afflictions right in the eye and tell them to go straight to hell! There is no place in your life for fear! Our afflictions no longer having power! For the next 10 days, we will focus on our dreams, hopes, goals and aspirations. READY? SET? GO!

Day 21

If you could live anywhere in the world, where would you live and why? Why aren't you living there now? What obstacles would you face in moving? What would you have to leave behind? Why wouldn't you want to leave these things behind?

_____
_____
_____
_____
_____
_____
_____
_____
_____
_____

Renita Johnson

The Attic

_____
_____
_____
_____
_____

MEDITATION

This writing exercise helps you to realize the things that have you bound. Take a good look at those things. Are they worth holding on to? If they are people, would they allow you to hold them from moving and going where they want to go? Evaluate those things. Now if you said you'd want to live in Hawaii (which is not that far-fetched) you may face other obstacles in getting there. This writing exercise isn't to say that you should just drop everything and move (unless you feel inclined to), but instead, it sheds light on the things in life you view as an obstacles.

Day 22

If a magic genie suddenly appeared and granted you three wishes, what would you wish for and why?

MEDITATION

After you get done, review your three wishes. Do you really need a magic genie to grant them, or is there something you could do to make your wishes a reality?

Day 23

What would be a perfect day for you? Write about what would take place in that day from the moment you got out of bed, to the moment you got back into bed.

MEDITATION

What would life be like if every day was like this day? Do you really want perfection? Would you be able to handle it? Life is not perfect, and sometimes it is not perfection that we seek. Review your perfect day, how is it different from your everyday life? Does it have more peace? Is there love there? Do you have more time to enjoy the things you want to enjoy? Look for the underlining tone of your perfect day. What is it that you really want on a day-to-day basis?

Day 24

As a child, what did you want to be when you grew up? Why? What was so fascinating about this career?

MEDITATION

If you did not pursue this as an adult, why didn't you? What kept you from achieving this? What caused you to change your mind? Is it too late to do purse those dreams? As children, the sky was the limit. We did not allow anything to hold us back. Meditate on your thought process as a child. Something's in life require us to have a child-like faith. We have to believe the way we did when we were children, seeing no obstacles, only the opportunity to be great.

Day 25

What are your personal, financial, career, and family goals? List them and their importance to your life.

MEDITATION

 Review your goals. If you could only choose five goals to work on, which would you pick? Circle your choices. This is an exercise used by billionaire, Warren Buffett. The five goals that you circled are most important to you. They are the goals that you will honestly focus on and work towards the hardest. The rest, are just goals that worry you and keep you up at night. Forget about those other goals until you tackle your top five.

Day 26

Plan how you will tackle these five goals. What will you do daily towards working on them?

MEDITATION

Sometimes, things happen and hurt us so bad we lose sight of our visions, goals, and dreams. Make a plan to keep you focused. When you focus on these goals, everything else will subside.

Day 27

Make a list of 25 things you want to do before you leave this earth.

MEDITATION

Before Kesha passed, she made a bucket list. It included things she wanted to do before she died. The list taught me that there is so much to look forward to in life. Sometimes, we focus so much on the bad we forget to live.

Day 28

What if each month you were given enough money to live comfortably? What would you spend your life doing now that working for a living is not a concern?

MEDITATION

Whatever your answer was reveals what you are most passionate about in life. Some of us may work to provide, but if we could do something else we would. Review what you have written. How could you fit time in to do this often? Is there income to be made in your answer? Could it be a business opportunity?

Day 29

What are you thankful for? Write a list of everything you are thankful for?

The Attic

MEDITATION

Creating a spirit of gratitude helps you to focus on the positive things in life. It gives us the positive energy we need to better ourselves. Think back on that attic again. It was hard to see all the good stuff hidden when we were so focused on the negative. Strive daily to think about the things for which you are grateful.

Day 30

Reflect on the last 29 days. Did you enjoy the experience? What was easy? What was difficult? What obstacles did you face? What have you learned about yourself? How will you use this experience?

The Attic

MEDITATION
Congratulations! You have made it through 30 days of Cleaning out the Attic. Spend some time meditating on what you have learned about yourself. It should not end here! Take a few moments each day to meditate, write or do something relaxing. This keep your attic from becoming cluttered. When spring cleaning, we often realize that if we would have taken a little time each day to clean, we wouldn't have such a big job to do! Do not allow stuff to clutter in your attic. Clean-up daily! Your mind, body, and spirit will thank you for it!

Activity 1

Go with the Flow   **Date:** _____

Directions Poetry is a fun way to express yourself! Use the space below to write your own poem or freestyle. It can be about anything! 1, 2, 3, FLOW!

Title:
By:

Activity 2

My Life Story **Date:** _____

Directions Imagine someone wrote a book about your life. What would the cover look like? Get creative! Include a picture, title, and theme!

Activity 3

You are Pretty Darn Special! **Date:** _____

Directions Do you know what happened the day or year you were born? Use the Internet (Google) to search your birthday! Record your cool findings!

_____

_____

_____

_____

_____

_____

_____

Activity 4

Who Am I? **Date:** _____

Directions Use each letter of your name to write words that describe who you are. Write it in large letters. Feel free to use different colors to spice things up. Pull out a dictionary/thesaurus if you get stuck.

Ex. RENITA

Real **E**xcellent **N**atural **I**ntelligent **Th**oughtful **A**wesome

Activity 5

What's Your Perception? **Date:** _____

Directions On the left side, express what you think people see when they look at you. On the right side, express what you hope/wish people would see when they look at you. You can express yourself through words or pictures.

Activity 6

Your Opinion Matters! **Date:** _____

Directions *Turn on the television. Pretend you are a television show critic. Pick a show and write a short review about it.*

Was it good?

Did it have a central point or lesson?

What did you learn?

Would you watch it again?

What did it leave you confused about?

What would have made the show better?

Did you see anything that reminded you of your own life?

Activity 7

Love For Sale **Date:** _____

Directions   *Imagine Cupid assigned you the job of selling Love. Create an advertisement for Love. Include a slogan, theme, and price. Get creative!*

Certificate of Completion

Certificate of Completion

Awarded to

_____

For Completing
30 Days of Cleaning out The Attic

Presented this _____ day of _____, year _____
By
Renita Johnson

www.ingramcontent.com/pod-product-compliance
Lightning Source LLC
LaVergne TN
LVHW011913080426
835508LV00007BA/508

9 781941 749210